JUNE ARCHER

Yes! You Can.

A Children's Book of Inspiration

ILLUSTRATED BY THE ART OF JAMES E. WALKER

Discover, Enrich & Inspire

Yes! You Can
A Children's Book Of Inspiration

Written by **June Archer**
Illustrated by The Art of **James E. Walker**
Creative Design by **James E. Walker & June Archer**

ISBN: 978-19358839-8-2
© 2017 Augustus Publishing, Inc.

UPTOWN Books January 2017
an imprint of **Augustus Publishing**

AugustusPublishing.com | UptownMagazine.com
113 East 125th street NY, NY, 10035

For

MAMA BEAR & MAGOO

THIS BOOK BELONGS TO:

_____

I AM _____ **YEARS OLD.**

Daddy, I don't know what I want to be when I grow up?

"You can be whatever you want to be. All you have to do is dream big!

Dreams do come true, all you have to do is believe!"

9

Can I be an architect and build tall skyscrapers?

Maybe I can be an airplane pilot and fly over tall buildings...

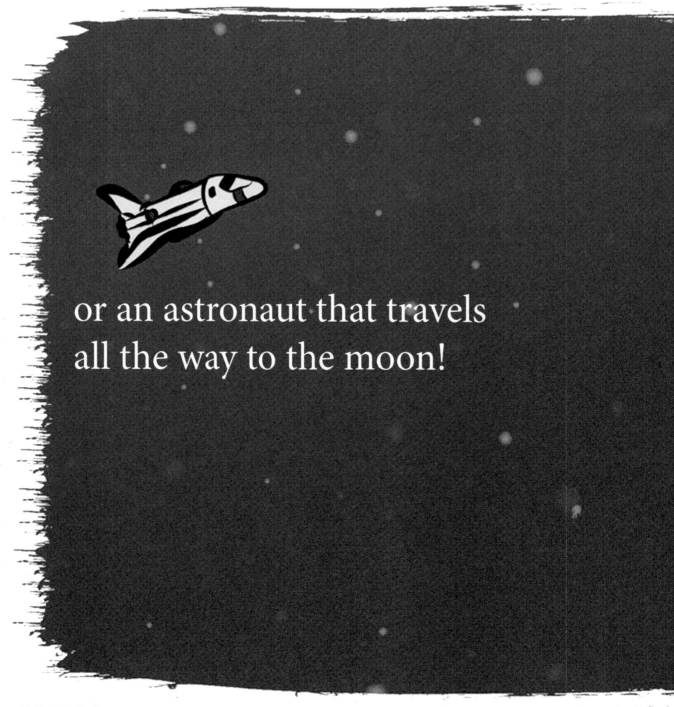

or an astronaut that travels
all the way to the moon!

Or how about a mail carrier, so I can deliver good news to people?

I would love to be a doctor so I can make people feel better!

What if I can be a musician and make music that people can dance to?

A teacher would be nice!
I could teach kids like me,
important things about history.

23

A comedian would be funny!
I like to make people laugh.

I could be a tennis player!

A baseball player!

I could even play golf!

Or maybe a fire fighter to help keep people safe.

I think I want to be an author, so I can tell people amazing stories.

How about a chef?
I can cook food that people
would love to taste?

When I grow up can I be a lawyer?

A fashion stylist?

How about the President of
The United States of America?

"Yes! You can.
You most certainly can!"

"You can be whatever
you want to be.
All you have to do
is dream big"

Dreams do come true,
all you have to do is believe!

This is to certify that I:

_____

(First Name)

Finished reading "Yes! You Can"
A Children's Book Of Inspiration.

When I Grow Up I Want To Be:

_____

I will be confident.
I will get good grades in school.
I will be nice to my friends and classmates.
I will respect my parents.
I can do anything in life as long as I work hard.

First Name: _____

Last Name: _____

SIGNED,

_____

Date:

**BUILDING THE
NEXT GENERATION
OF POSITIVE MINDS**

WORKSHEET
(Circle The Best Answer)

This person delivers the mail:

a) Astronaut

b) Mail Carrier

c) Police Officer

This person makes people eel better:

a) Stylist

b) The President

c) Doctor

This person puts out fires:

a) Fire Fighter

b) Actor

c) Golf Player

This person prepares food:

a) Baseball Player

b) Comedian

c) Chef

This person flies planes:

a) Architect

b) Pilot

c) Lawyer

If you are a Fire Fighter you use this:

a) Tennis racket

b) Space ship

c) Fire TruckYes!

When you play golf you need a:

a) Mail bag

b) Golf club

c) Baseball bat

If you were the President of
The United States, where would you live?

a) Connecticut

b) Hollywood

c) The White House

MAKERSPACE

A creative platform for young thinkers and future leaders.

Color in a character or Draw your favorite character that you like from the book

MAKERSPACE

A creative platform for young thinkers and future leaders.

Color in a character or Draw your favorite character that you like from the book

MAKERSPACE

A creative platform for young thinkers and future leaders.

Color in a character or Draw your favorite character that you like from the book

MAKERSPACE

A creative platform for young thinkers and future leaders.

Color in a character or Draw your favorite character that you like from the book

Color in a character or Draw your favorite character that you like from the book

JUNE ARCHER is the President & CEO of **Eleven28 Entertainment Group**, a premier music and social media marketing company in Hartford, Connecticut.

Go beyond the pages of YES! YOU CAN.

Join the Yes! Community!
IAm**JuneArcher**.com

www.Facebook.com/YesEverydayCanBeAGoodDay!
Twitter / Instagram / Pinterest / YouTube: @JuneArcher!

Books By **June Archer**

Yes! Everyday Can Be A Good Day
The keys to success that lead to an amazing life

Yes! You Can
A children's book of inspiration

After You Say, **Yes!**
The keys to living an amazing life with the one you love
